DK READERS

LEARNING
pre-level
1
TO READ

Fishy Tales

A Dorling Kindersley Book

Take a
swim in the
blue sea.

snorkel

clam

Here is a
coral reef.

 coral

What can you see?

coral

fish

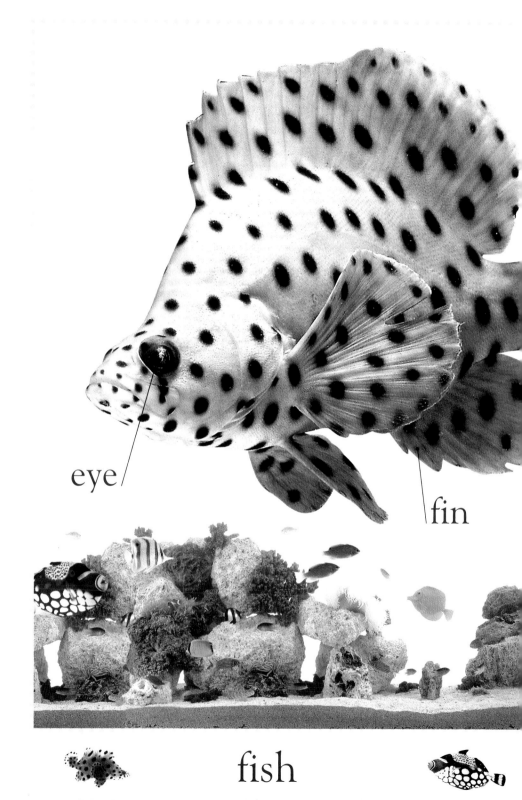

eye

fin

fish

spot

Small fish
are swimming
in and out
of the coral.

The turtles are playing in the sea.

shell

 turtles

flipper

tail

sea horses

fin

snout

The sea horses
are swaying
to and fro.

arm

 starfish

Starfish
are crawling
on the seabed.

tentacles

jellyfish

Jellyfish
are floating
up and down
in the sea.

bell

17

fin

tail

Here comes a shark
looking for food.

sharks

mouth

octopuses

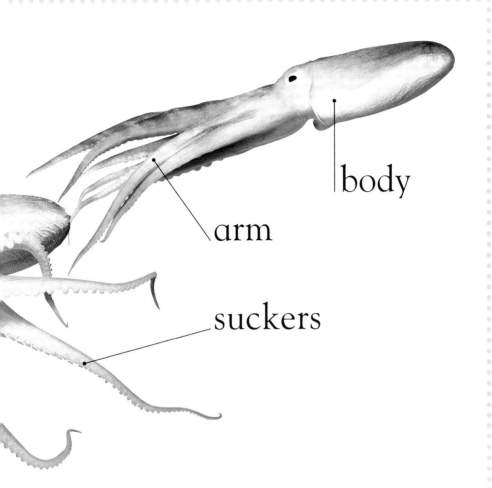

body

arm

suckers

An octopus is
zooming off
to hide.

claw

crabs

leg

Crabs are hiding
in the coral and
in big shells.

shell

tail

A ray is hiding
on the seabed.

rays

eye

fin

25

A dolphin is
swimming away
from the shark.

mouth

dolphins

tail

flipper

Eels are
looking
out for
the shark.

tail

eels

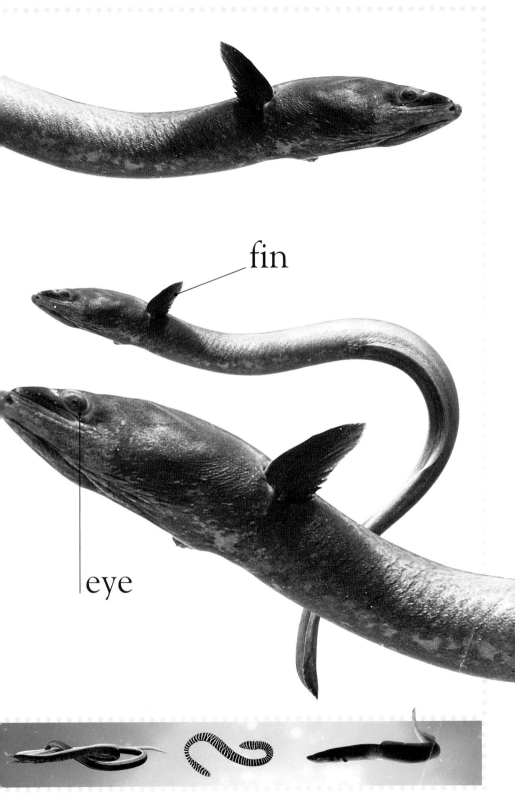

fin

eye

29

The shark is
swimming away.

Can you see ...

Picture word list

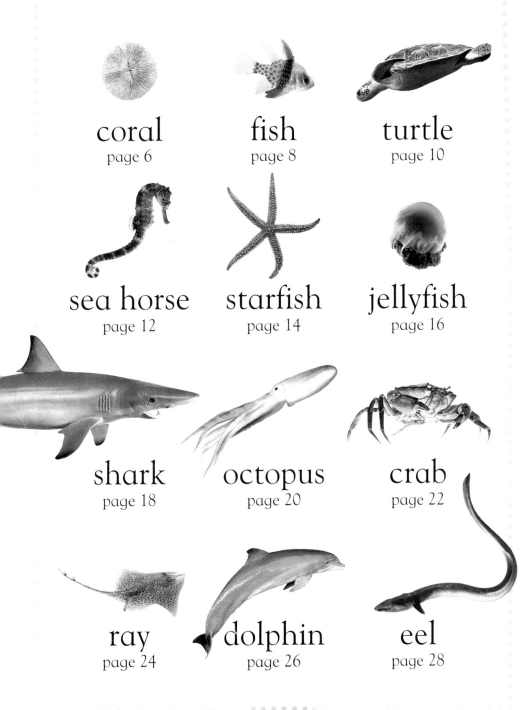

coral
page 6

fish
page 8

turtle
page 10

sea horse
page 12

starfish
page 14

jellyfish
page 16

shark
page 18

octopus
page 20

crab
page 22

ray
page 24

dolphin
page 26

eel
page 28

fin

gills

nose

a fish ![fish] ? coral ![coral] ?